# MASTER BEDROOM POEMS

# Master Bedroom Poems

SANDRA AGRICOLA

*An Ohio Review Book*
*Athens, Ohio*

Published by THE OHIO REVIEW, Athens, Ohio 45701–2979

Several of these poems have previously appeared in magazines as follows: in THE OHIO REVIEW, "On A Wide Bed" and "State of Grace"; in the *AWP Newsletter,* "The Wanderer"; in *The Chariton Review,* "Chit-Chat"; in *The Denver Quarterly,* "Courting Grandaddy Longlegs" and "Domestication of Flies". Also several poems were included in the chapbook "Dark and Short and Wildly Pink," published by THE OHIO REVIEW.

Library of Congress Cataloging in Publication Data

Agricola, Sandra.
Master Bedroom Poems.

(Ohio Review Books)

I. Title.

PS3551.G74M37 1985 811'.54 85–28550

ISBN 0–942148–05–3
ISBN 0–942148–04–5 (pbk.)

Cover photo by Jack Agricola
Cover design by Jack Keely
Design by Karla Stover
Set in 11 point Bembo by Chappel Typesetting
Manufactured in the U.S.A.
Publication of this book has been aided by a grant from the Ohio Arts Council.

for my family
past, present, future

## Contents

### I

II

I

## *Backsliding*

I woke this morning and dreamed the seasons
had set themselves in reverse.
Fall becomes summer and I toss out dark
fevers like chunks of week-old meat.

The rain begins and Dutch bulbs
placed in the cellar fall from their shelves
and burst into bloom. It is spring and the whirl
of rot and rebirth is a rhyme I sing to myself
when the garden is hopeless. Jack and Jill
touch crowns, touch crowns.

Touch the soft spot under my ear.
You can hear my heart.
If you press there it will stop.

When my father siphoned gas
out of one tank to fill another
what was I thinking?
Of the nozzle? The delicious-smelling
vapor traveling uphill? Suck and Spit.

It is against every law of nature.

Any morning I could wake to find myself dead.

## *Gently Sinking*

It wasn't a good year.
Even though my brother's girlfriend
went to the prom with tiny daisies in her hair
and I thought she must be the prettiest girl alive.
We knew it wasn't because that year the Elberta peaches
rotted under the trees.
The man who sang Are You Safe in the Arms of Jesus?
died in his sleep. They told us the
needle marks covered his body.
Even under his toenails, even
between the pale webs of his fingers
that played the electric guitar
to make you scream Yes I am
safe. Even if you knew you had come close
to a smell like chlorine and to a night
dark and short and wildly pink:
My brother's best friend breaks naked
into a stubborn pond that will not yield
and will not dry up. Bloated and happy,
he will not surface for weeks.

## *Wishbone*

I feel my stomach rejecting this food.
Hardboiled eggs swallowed whole,
like advice, in one ear and, *voilà*,
an egg protrudes from my father's mouth.
He smiles. So calm, he balances a bowl of food
and waits.

Beautiful carcass I have become,
I cannot sit at the same table with them.
Father smiles.
Sister accepts another helping.
It is not wise to eat your fill.

I recite silently
French phrases my body obeyed
long ago: *plié, pas de deux,* my knees go out
like broken tools.
This dance is difficult.
I could spend my whole life perfecting it:
hold, hold, *hold.*

I take what father offers:
almost love, we pull the wishbone,
sucked clean, two unequal parts.

# *Lean River*

1

The beautiful loaves and fishes story
told to us on Sunday morning.
Anyone could do it inside church,
so close to God and shadows
cast by his image,
the miracle in silhouette.

Home again, away from God's majesty,
it wasn't so easy to divide
and multiply into infinity.
Easier to illustrate than analyze
exactly how many times five thousand
will go into two.
The bountiful fish would be small,
a decimal point on the tongue.

2

Every Sunday he came home sunburned
and drunk with one or two
small-mouth bass
stiff as Archibald's knuckles
against his wife's iron bed.
Like taking a bullet in the gut—
the mouth, in its last shape, says *No!*

*Leaning into the big one,*
*the one that pulled and tugged*
*until everything snapped,*
*Daddy pulled out his naked lady deck*
*thumbed and watermarked*

*from watching everything go down*
*and reappear again*
*unmanned.*

3

How I loved this man.
Silver jitterbugs hung in his hat
like stars and mama cried.
On those nights we were almost happy—
as sad as grits and gray salmon from a can.

Glasses clinking and mama weeping.
His face red as hell,
allergic and sore,
sullen as her nightgown
hanging behind the bathroom door.

4

Next morning Daddy took me to a mountain
and held me on his shoulders.
We could see three states,
four if he lifted me
into thin air.
The mountain store sold chocolate ants,
rattlesnake soup and pickled eggs.
Anything was possible on top of that mountain—
life, liberty, the pursuit of wildness.
Nobody was ever hungry for anything.

# *Chit Chat*

I'm going to tell you the same story
until I get it straight.
It's summer.
Not a sound playing on the water
just light
brilliant in its complex and troubled state.
I can almost count the words between us
since Mama's death.
Furniture styles and hairstyles,
a few misplaced loves,
and recently
words about babies and bank vaults,
sweet potato recipes
and husbands.
Just words. Enough of this *chit chat*
you say. I'm tired of it.

I'm going to tell you the same story
over and over.
It's always summer.
And your father's first daughter
is suddenly sharing your bed.
I'm afraid of everything new
and so are you. Afraid
I will brush against you as I sleep.
You are afraid to leave the house,
afraid I might take your place.
I can imagine you running back in,
hair damp from play, and all of us saying
Who is that little girl with the auburn hair?
She doesn't belong here anymore.

There's not a sound in this house, in this new dark.
We lie beside each other and wait
for the floor to open up and swallow me,
put everything back like it was.
Then the monster in the master bedroom
begins his music.
Nasal snore, arrogant and selfish.
How could he?
How could he disturb our small and silent world,
an unconscious reptile
responsible for everything wrong
in our lives.

I'm going to tell you the same old story.
It's summer again.
There's not a sound on the water
just light.
Brilliant and too complex to comprehend
beneath the surface.

I have a feeling things are about to change
again. The lull after lunch.
Mama broke an egg into the meatloaf
and there were two yolks.
Perfectly formed
sucked in and out of her hands
to make something new and not very pretty.
If you want something filling
you have to sweat it.
The stove heats up the whole house.
This evening a red-headed woodpecker
found himself trapped inside our porch.

Screeching and chattering to find a way back to his family.
The mother hunched against him on the other side
as though warmth was everything, as though
she understood that beneath all that surface chit-chat
was love— inarticulate and sometimes swollen
beyond recognition.

Tree frogs fill the gullies tonight.
They sing *heart, heart, heart.*
Flat on my stomach, I wake,
jerking my feet inside the covers.
I know how easy it is to trade places,
finding the comfortable bed gone,
turning on every light and finding nothing
because, after so much time spent in darkness,
it hurts to look.
There is something very orderly about displacement:
one dead cow equal to so much damp earth,
nothing more.
Any deep hole fills quickly with water and larvae,
nothing more.

## *Master Bedroom*

I've inhaled the past as though it were steam
escaping,
an old-fashioned pressure cooker about to blow
its cap, spewing its contents shamelessly
in all directions.
I've collected secrets
perhaps someday to figure out
why they must not be told.

My best friend's father scattered himself
all over the master bedroom,
sky-high and eternally gone
in the middle of April, 2:15,
a glorious day for a nap,
the old shotgun asleep beside him—
innocent and warm.
We were at school watching Gene Matthews
scrape his fingernails across the blackboard,
the marks of an ancient turtle
trapped and determined
to find his way out again.
Squeals and screaming,
ears covered, teeth gone brittle.

She never mentioned him again.
Her mother bought a new rug, unsoiled and unpatterned
with the past, and started sewing furiously.
We lay in the sun sucking ice
a few feet from the room,
the old Singer stopping and starting,
starting up again like our hearts

whenever we thought about Gene Matthews
or large breasts.
We tried to burn ourselves off the face of the earth.
It didn't work. We always came back when the ice wore out.

Christ, she was beautiful.
She was suffering.
I'd watch her at night sitting up in bed,
a sack of lemons and some salt.
She sucked them till the enamel gave way,
lips pursed, tongue moving desperately
over what was missing.

## *As Always, Summer*

Baby goats dance on their hind legs
gathering plums
almost ripe.
The field is plump yellow,
the road's edge is red,
clover red, good luck red.
And in the distance a silo
with part of its head blown off,
like a man pushing his hat back, scratching,
wondering what the shit has gone wrong
on a day like today.

Uncalled for, unbearable weather
has brought the bitches into heat.
All over the neighborhood
they are chasing after one dark spot
or another. Male following male following
God knows what deep down aroma.
Walking home I see a dog
humped by another, both male.
They're so exhausted and so happy to be so
that by now
to roll around with other losers
in mud and grass is good enough.

The ground was hard as steel
but I cracked it open,
an affair of the heart,
and searched for bulbs
placed deep in the ground
on a hill behind our house.
The crocus bulbs were hollow.
Even the worms which had crawled inside them

for life— hollow.
And the worm crap, too,
hollow.

In Mississippi
ants multiply so fast it's dangerous
to walk around barefoot.
They have raised the dead
and carried it back for their queen.
It is a miraculous sight.

## *Scarecrows*

Placing my hands under his trousers
I push the stake deeper
to try and save him.
Jesus on stilts.
The starlings love this man.
They have pecked his face to shreds.

I take off his watch,
unhook his gold cross.
A child's body now,
a grass whistle wet and frail.
Without desire.

This is passion—
I shout at the fat nurses
who draped this body
as they would cover a table
full of old food.
Nothing must show—the flies.

The sun loses its place and slides
out of sight, slick and undressed.
A rainbow starling opens her beak
skyward and blue to catch it.

## *Long Shots*

1

We lost the trifecta.
Our long shot broke stride in the final stretch.
How could we know?
She sat serenely drinking gin,
smooth skirt covered with owls.
In four months she would be dead.

In the slaughtering yards of heaven
she is one of the losers playing pool
at the right hand of God and Michelangelo.
Clever, she knows how to win without winning.
Her cue ball against the eight ball slides
head-first into an uncalled pocket.

These are the nightmares of the dead:
her teeth were perfect when she died.
Mine throb.
She watches her daughter lie awake,
a dull, dry ache.

2

Poppies and tulips are growing
out of my mother's grave.
I did not plant them and no one
else did either. It is as though
she held her breath
through the snow and rain and now
is exhaling slowly, warmly.

I have dug the flowers and found no bulbs.
The man I love waits in the car
two nights before a wedding.
I can touch nerves tonight.
Here, above my mother's grave
and there, in the tight outline of
his body waiting, wondering
what he's got himself into.

## *Sweet Williams*

In my mother's house china kewpie dolls touch.
If I pull them apart, they bob and sway
on a worn-out spring. No way out but back
together so I leave them as I left them
twenty years ago, eyes closed
kissing.

Her window is open and we watch
the curtains with sweet williams,
God's saddest flower, rock in and out of the heat.
Her life is almost over.
I dance in a black skirt,
spinning under glass like the Lalique fish
in Sam Jackson's gift shop.

I am sorry for everything
I never did right.
She is forgiving me again,
pushing a sack of pecans at me
as if to say *You may need these*
*and you'll have them.*

The days are so hot in Georgia
you can fry an egg on the sidewalk.
At least that's what we used to say.
That's why the rooms are so big and dark.

## *Of Grief*

All, by some miracle,
swept away as cleanly and carefully
as a magician's kerchief covers first
this hand and then the other.
A huge eclipse of sun and moon.

I said a prayer, walked home in the rain
and couldn't remember when the cancer started
or which doctor to blame for finishing
his dinner of Japanese raw fish and saying
mother was too far gone for anything
but comfort.

All I remember is underthings.
Will she need panties?
Do they bury them barefoot?
I still don't know.

## *Fish Market*

The dead eye gaze of a cold, gray flounder.
Mama stops, pinches her nose together
as though refusing her supper, fishy already
in the top of her bag. She clutches her scarf,
the knot it makes under her chin, and tries to turn
me toward the waves swollen up like pride.

The Gulf of Mexico surrenders itself to the shore,
teasing the land with starfish and pale cameos
that sink deep and unredeemable by morning.
The market is all eyes, all ice. The man behind
the counter slices a catfish lengthwise,
walks over glass shells, sounds of old
arguments and divorce.

Outside, Mama holds me and spreads the moon's
stubborn light. Silver light
like a pocketful of old change. She rubs my head.
I understand these moods. I rest my head
against her chest and say nothing.

These are the nights of the iguana
soft and cold on her pillow. These are
the nights when making it alone seems impossible.
When she needs a man and sends me to bed early.

We walk the stairs quickly and
Mama fixes a milkshake for the two of us.
She opens a bottle of vanilla.
She is in her slip. I am closing all the curtains
again. The foam around the mouth is always the best

part and we laugh in spite of ourselves.
The catfish smile like us, even in
someone else's arms.

## *The Body Can't Heal Itself*

Blistered and cracked from the weight of me,
my feet won't carry this miracle,
myself, much longer.
I sit on the edge of the tub—
yin and yang    sun and moon
blossomed out of season
and pick the skin from my feet.
A slave
tired of cotton and stooping
and her own dark feet.
The last time I was peeling away skin
was Florida.
Soaking up the sun's glamour,
pulling at my own body
as if to find the mystery on the surface—
give and take of the sun.

Mama told me she took all her babies
to the Little Giant Supermarket
and had the butcher weigh us on his scales.
That doesn't seem right.
There's too much blood around,
too much discarded.

I've bought all the suggested creams.
Those that prevent stretch marks
and others that soothe the ones already
tattooed and fawning for more attention.
Cream for sore nipples and jellies
for rashes and the circumcised penis.
And that doesn't seem right either—
that the body can't heal itself,

that atmosphere can go from bad to worse sometimes
and never heal at all
and not always forever.
And the sun goes right on,
drying up and drying up.
Not a care.

# *Annunciation and Two Naked Youths*

A woman on the front row
wears a wide-brimmed red
hat like the one the Pope wears
when he visits Africa and walks
the beaches barefoot, almost real.
She is not Catholic but she sits here anyway
mesmerized by the priest who folds and unfolds
his sermon like a yo-yo: damned, undamned. The flowers
thirsting above her head
remind her of her own dilemma.
Something is missing.
She watches her open-toe sandals,
her stomach still flat, still whole.
The minister is chanting again
but this is not a bullfight. But
because the church is so hot, because he
swerves to accept the collection plate
and coins crash against bronze like
a noisy *coup de grace*
she tosses her hat high and shouts
*Olé!* We shouldn't laugh.
After all there was Mary sitting
quietly with a handkerchief in her lap.
The Hallelujah chorus was one silk handkerchief
flung high over her shoulder when Gabriel entered
the picture out of some blind alley.
Perhaps she worried for months
about the possibility of twins.
How would she explain to Joseph
that God had made a mistake.
That the bloody bull sweats with fear
long after the heart has given up.

## *Small Bones*

1

It is leap year again
and wood burns quickly through the extra day.
There's a child to think about
so I place another log on
and throw the dampers wide.

His skin is still so tender,
so new and unaccustomed,
the wind chaps and stings whatever I leave exposed,
the carelessness of uninvited elements.
So I cover everything
until only his eyes are visible
blue and wild as the sea of dreams.

It is warm today
and I have released him to the world
for awhile.
But I know he will come back too soon,
before I am finished with the same unfinished business.
Pressing his face against the screen,
*See. Come see.*
I follow him outside to see forgotten passions
taking shape in something new.

2

A loggerhead drops her eggs, covers them
in sand and struts out to sea in brilliant darkness.
Soon there are too many to count
making their way

air-raid fashion
back to shining sea.

The males will never return to land
and neither male nor female remembers
the slick underside of her,
the cushion of skin protecting life
mosaic of small bones
breaking under the Atlantic floor,
surfacing thousands of years later
in the hands of a child too young to realize
he is fisted around a century or more.

3

The house is dirty and bright
with John
and bills that choke the dining room table,
unpaid. Unpayable.
Sitting here together it doesn't matter
how little we accomplish.
It's when I say goodnight
that I lie with myself again and tremble.

I kneel down with him to pray
for small miracles. For stray dogs
who patrol the moon's coming and going,
for sirens that work their way east and west
saving the world.
And for things to change—
to go coatless and free.
There's so much left to pray for

but I fall in bed agnostic
and silent as some old bullfrog who finally sees
the morning's light but doesn't know what to do about it.

Now I lay me down on cool sheets
and the ground is covered up with frost.
Safe bird, I do not care who comes in
and sees me in the blue bedroom
with bluebird pictures on the wall,
room for not one more in here,
my heart grows so fat in this bed
waiting
pumping big as a tomato
I put on my head like a Mexican peasant
I had my picture taken with.

It does not hurt so bad
when I can hold my work: my son: my heart
like fruit gone bad
away from my body.

Then the cold rain sweeps the house,
the trees begin their sad song,
my son cries out for something else
I can never provide.

# II

# *Armadillo*

Shade is what you kill for
in the South. It makes a woman crazy
when every day she cannot relax and every night
she cannot get close to her husband
unless she soaks in a cold tub, head against
green porcelain.
It does not matter so much if she ever
comes clean, just so long as the body
can calm down and lie flat as plankton.

The long wave of heat slithers across the road,
folds itself around an azalea bush
where yesterday the children found a possum,
hunched and stiff, and circled it
to learn the wide-eyed meaning of fear:

a rooster with spurs long as a marlin spike
circles a hen in the darkened dew of morning.

I'd like to turn away.

The blue-eyed shell of an armadillo
cornered under the steps and the flesh of it,
the dark muscled flesh of it, thrown
near the shore for everyone to walk around,
washes clean as new moon.

## *One Minute You're Dead to the World*

I close mother's velour robe around my body and
sparks fly from my legs and waist,
stationary charges stored for centuries
over the insulated.
It is cold in this house.
The coffeepot sweats above the flame,
sweats and tries to keep warm.
I lean against the stairs and wait.

At the back of my neck I feel it.
A certain coldness that cannot
be rubbed away. As though the glands
all over my body refused the curious hand
that wants to make everything better again.

And when there is nothing else to say
we build a fire.
We hold our hands over the black stove
so long we can't feel the heat
or the room growing tighter as it warms.

## *Viscera*

In Georgia a farmer gutted a pig
behind his house and let the blood
form pools around it,
thick as mineral water. It was a good day for it—
smooth shoulder, strong arch, deep full hams.

And she remembers her father's trousers,
the sweet smell of guts
when she tried to rub the stiff legs to pieces
before hanging them in a steady breeze.
(Whisper Chattahoochee, I've got to get away)

Nothing suits her.
Not the baby shad scattering against her feet
or the string of bream
her husband hangs in front of her
like a trophy but not a trophy,
another fish to fry up crisp,
pick bones from meat.

The scalings cover her arms,
the white counters, the glazed sink.
From the dining room the man smells Clorox,
sits looking out the window till the sun
falls in his lap. He takes his plate in to her.
It is dry now. One sliced Vidalia onion too many.

Whisper Chattahoochee when tree frogs sing,
when she is all alone.
She pulls out a bag of coins:
Kennedy's smooth lips, the worn torso

of a Spanish lady dancing, always dancing.
Her back laced tightly, the rest of her
flowing like a blue-green river.

# *On a Wide Bed*

We fish the car bodies today.
Dark Walleyes flirt with us.
Gregarious and greedy, they will not dine
on our leftovers but leave us hanging in a '63 Impala
corroded and alive with fish.
After so much frustration
still
we are happy.

At night ripe fish move over sand and gravel
discharging glass-eyed eggs,
lifting and darning their gills
just out of reach.
Marriage is like this.
The feeling that everything good
lies somewhere just beyond the everyday.
Lurking in shadows,
white and tender flesh.

Drunk on a wide bed
wondering how it all began
our teeth are stained and glowing.
This
is our natural state.
We aren't always this passive
or spend this much time
trying to end up in each other's arms.
Most of the time we don't even need arms.

And yet
in this condition

we are in love.
Fragile as carp
growing on the water's surface,
rootless and pale.

## *The Chore of Death*

1

Leaving the pond to catch
fish in the salt marshes,
the alligators.
They are in no kind of hurry.
If it takes all night
let it.
They're just hungry.
They swallow too many
and swallow
and then get a stomach ache and
want to go back home.
Along the way they pause,
reconsider,
rest on one another's back,
bloated together like medieval armor.
They're just hungry.
They just follow a well-used path.
All of nature is sick
at the sight of them,
the way they surface,
all at once, splitting
the moon's idiot face
for fish, for fish,
for fish.

2

I wait for the men at the stables
and hear the lean
liver-colored dogs long
before I see them switchback

through dry grass song.
They each have two,
maybe three, gray quail
in their saddlebags.
Not worth cleaning.
We'll clean them anyway.
The dogs howl to go again.
We could run them to
death and then regret it.
Mother is standing at the sink with a small
bird's head between her fingers.
A rosary, the chore of death,
the likes of which the world
has never felt, full of grace and
grain and shot.

3

A horse collapsed in the stable
tonight, and it's almost more stillness
than any of us has ever seen.
Sheer weight and blackness.
And the quail, so airy
by comparison that you can kill
one-two-three and never notice
the woods grown less dense.
I am in the kitchen with
quail scattered across the kitchen
table. I hear them starting the tractor.
It's the only way they know to overcome it.
To push it over a cliff and hope
they can scrape up enough dirt to cover it.

4

I spent the first half of my life,
my mother tells me,
just trying to get enough
clothes and meat on my bones.
I can't remember what I've been doing
the last half. Sometimes I feel half
human, half nothing at all.
Just hot and lazy.
A fan at each end of the room,
oscillating,
moves the same air over
the same area at least a thousand
times per hour.
Alone. In the middle of
who knows what cycle, I lie down.
Very still.
Near an open window.
I don't belong to anything.
I am so gentle, Jesus
should carry me away from this
air before somebody hurts me.

## *State of Grace*

I believe in one God, maker of man and woman,
of plus and minus, of porous and nonporous.
My body has become a sieve that filters desire
and disease and holy light.
I now understand the celibate—
hold me in your arms
nothing escapes from me but the tasteless gas of heaven.

In this priesthood
we are all closing our robes around us
like vestments someone else has ironed.
We are all becoming everlasting

works of art. Degas' plump dancer,
muscle-bound Sibyl, all
very becoming
even in disaster's unavoidable wake,
the night before Easter when the altar is stripped

of its cloth and finery. We are all waiting
for the return of everything. We don't want to die
on the night he was betrayed or any other night
but especially not now with everything standing
wide open and empty. We are on shallow waters

scooping the rainbow trout with our bare hands.

It is Spring
and the pressure of our touch
causes it to urinate clouds of fertile eggs.
We hold the second coming in our hands.

I sit in a bathtub up to my armpits,

a washcloth draped over my breasts.
Now I'm the Mona Lisa, sifting murky water,
stroking the bones of my feet with lanolin and rosemilk,
waiting to be scooped up tail and all.

## *Courting Grandaddy Longlegs*

Where we live you can't get rid of them,
might as well learn
this is what you live with.
At night they begin their long
legged journey toward the comfort
of one another.
On the clapboards,
in the sink,
around the sacred shower,
finally climbing in bed with us.
Immaculate bed, immaculate body.
Like threads on some ragged blanket
they are here.
Just legs. Legs
and legs and a pinpoint of nothing,
the essence of nothing, a harmless nest of
body and legs.

Like pubic hair
rich in its abundance
spiraling into desire
and no and no
and rarely yes.
It's what we put up with day after day.
It doesn't get any better
and it never takes a turn for the worse.
A net that takes my breath
as it covers this house like some huge lie.
No matter how clean everything seems on the surface,
you can't escape it
and no one can save you.

## *Domestication of Flies*

Rain all morning and the lake is silver and gray.
On the surface, stretch marks are all
that holds this lake within its banks.
Imperfections only the sun can heal
and it does again and again
as though it, too, is ashamed
of the violent side of life.

Rain all evening and the spider's web
sparkles under the eaves.
She will work all night on this murderous
quilt and in the morning no one,
not even a fly,
will notice . . . .

Washing up, washing this green silky shell,
that blue-green cape, flying off
then landing in the same spot,
getting nowhere, impatient
to be clean for courting
behind the brassy yellow light.
Washing up again afterwards
modestly this time.
I am the sudden intruder,
an inhuman eavesdropper
as she rubs her legs, adjusts her sheer stocking-like
wings behind the parchment-colored dressing lamp.

Now they are beginning to annoy—
fussing at each other, flying
into—then making up,
talking at once, interrupting

saying nothing—whispering sing-song
gossip. Deferring each to the other's
buzzing hymn of desire.

But I will not slap them around tonight.
Or pin them between light and shade.

Not tonight.
They are too eager to please.

## *The Heart, A Natural Shape*

I came all the way
to see you today. Started back home once,
but the damn cows wouldn't budge.
They drove me back where I was headed.
Mooing at me pumping furiously
on a bicycle without wheels
to you.

I leaned hard into the traffic,
my body touching the handlebars,
becoming one with the idea of fright.
A dangerous incline.
My muscles working as hard to stop
as they had to start
all this momentum.

Most of the time in stories like this
one or the other would have been there
and gone already, the climax of missed connections.
When I arrived you were there too.
We wandered the store picking postcards.
Beautiful souvenirs
that seemed to dance with natural neon
and pale coral
growing and growing deeper
and deeper into pinkness, the heart
a natural shape that longs to be recognized
in out of the way places.

## *The Wanderer*

1

The sun is behaving like any middle
aged star. Shedding its debris,
puffing up
and then losing weight,
eclipsing what is left of the moon's
new skin
and misbehaving terribly
by wandering out of sight forever.

2

I have studied the sun's behavior
and I believe this is how a galaxy dies.
First the notion of divinity passes
away. Then dark moles erupt
all over the sun's face.
Even Prometheus is afraid to
visit this old light.
Wispy filaments of silver gas
explode and trail behind it
like hair, uncontrollable.
Useless.
It is ashamed and wants to hide behind the moon
which has grown big and burly again.

3

The molecules of my body are as tightly packed
as dirt

as cheese hidden away in a barrel.
When I begin dying it will take years
before anyone notices.
Afterwards, I fall apart dryly.
Pale, then gray, then murky brown.
The sun dies in beautiful rings of color
that fly madly through available space.
The whole world will know of its disappearance.
We will think the universe is expanding,
pulling our hearts along with it.
Dogs rise up out of the monkey grass
wondering why it has grown so cold.
Eyes can't adjust to this much darkness.

# *Retrieving Skeletons*

1

Nobody dared read them.
Nobody read anything.
They just listened between silence
and sleep for more static and a return
to normality.

They were intimidating.
I don't know why they worried me so—
hundreds of READER'S DIGEST lying
on tables and shelves of the Seaside Hospital.
Pastel covers of isolated beaches,
lighthouses,
wildlife.

More wildlife.

So much inspiration that goes unheeded
even in the face of new danger.
New warnings—
artificial respiration,
the hazards of exposed wires,
how someone's life is saved,
miraculously,
by someone else's prayers.

We were all waiting to be saved,
waiting for the cycle to end
as calmly as if it were a load of clothes
and we the bored few who still hang out in laundromats.

My parents used to receive them

in brown paper wrappers,
as if they were reading something too filthy
for the postman to lay eyes on.
They stacked them on the living room table
beside the plastic dome where
it was always winter inside
and the deer always survived the sudden and violent
storm.

2

The sun has returned, a pregnant bitch
who drags herself across the yard
after everyone else has given up.
The coffee, too, is weak this morning.
It won't keep me going past noon.
There's not much left of me
except too much open air.

From the boats I hear country music
and smell ripe fish and sweet varnish.
Two black labradors have been retrieving fish heads
all morning. They drop the skulls at my feet,
sneeze sand from their nose and sneeze some more
just for the strange feel of it.

Space is what you notice on the heads.
What should be there is washed away
or sucked clean by sun and dogs.
What you notice is the pink body
that isn't here.
And what you wonder is how it happened,

how long it floated blind
before warm sand took over
filing away flesh and color and kind.

3

There is an obvious reason for all this:
Nature made a mistake and let everything die.
Even the sun is having trouble making up his mind:
to go or stay, to illuminate or vanish completely.
Funny fat body.
Such dark peace. Peace and tranquility.

The land looks so startled.
Exposed and protected from nothing.
The sky is the color of sky.
Everything seems so dirty,
so fishy and soiled. Used-up.
We should wrap the land in brown paper
then walk away forever.
That'll teach it to mess around on us.

# *Cold Exalted*

I tire easily and go to bed early.
I wake up coughing
late at night or early in the morning.
Who knows?
My watch is just some hole
on my wrist—black on black against black
in this dark room. The moon's face uplifted
out there somewhere and everywhere—
Where?
I keep bumping my face against nothing
but walls, and doors I thought I'd left open.

The cold out the window is warm.
I am far away from it now.
Between me and it is everything
I can't get rid of— family, darkness,
glass. The glare off the snow scorches.
This is no ordinary cold, and I,
no ordinary woman. I am *Yeti,*
the snowman the world lost,
melting into the sheets,
making a mess of things again.

I sit up in bed, coughing up
the terror of sleep,
another dry-land dream I pull away from
before the climax.
My underwear is missing again.
Wet spots small as dimes.
I reach for Chloraseptic,
a green mist and everything goes numb—
the roof, the cavity, the other clit
hanging between here and eternity.

Nothing is transcendent.
In the morning the wet spots will be gone
and so will I.
They do not shine around me—
the body's constellation.

## *Sugar Ditch*

*for the people of Tunica, Mississippi*

Tonight I open my mouth to blackness
black cave of my mouth    black sky
and feel what tree ferns go through
when they die and resurrect wet-green
and glorious—the beyond is beyond
color
absence of white

Stuttering light    throbbing earth
this is no way to live
or die
beside a ditch in Mississippi
without hope
sweet as sugar toast
melted butter and sugar on top
and that is all you git
just enough
to make you water for more

This is no way to live
beside a ditch in
Mississippi
that gives of sewer lace
and feces
sweet as cream

No way to die
hungry
tail tucked between your legs
like a frightened crawfish
flat on his back

eyes rolled back
to see the pine trees
sing a little in the breeze
all swaying together
like no other tree on earth
free at last—
back and forth then back in place
like they never moved
and then the rain
clean and slow and badly needed
like everything else in Mississippi.

## *Divine Intervention*

Sartre said nausea is an image of
our unconsciousness.

So when I adjusted my socks today and
smelled the dark squid of my body,
I wasn't dirty
I was thinking how the night is no good,
how it oozes black and soft.
How all the summer nights
are like soft-shell crabs
sliced and savored until you are sick and
you want to go home slowly
until the love is out of your system.

I was thinking about God.
How on the seventh day he rested.
He's finished with us—a soft-shell crab
which abandons a piece of himself to the cool green
comfort below. Free at last.
Water and slime running between His joints and divine muscles.

I lie down with a lover
beside still waters.
He worships every part of me.
And when the sun goes down
we peel shrimp
and suck crawfish.
Our flesh smells of garlic and gumbo,
stew the angels gave Mary
when she was weak and bleeding,
Jesus at her breast.

It makes me ill,
this concoction of cloudy soup
so rich and yet so watered down
by centuries of simmering and cooling off,
adding to and taking away.

I take a lover
between flannel sheets paisley and spotted
with all manner of beasts
extinct and forgotten.
We smell of garlic and perch
smothered in red wine.
Sleep, finally.
Drunk and worn out from blessing
so much flesh,

we keep floating to the top.
And God, disgusted and tired
still
after countless centuries
refuses, refuses, refuses.

# *Interfacing*

If we're not careful, we'll lose everything
everyday.
A way our mind has of warning us, vivid pictures
of spoils after disaster
before the real disaster strikes.
Like those Christmas balls your mother handed you—
fragile and bright—she had seen the sharp fragments
seconds before trusting you with them and warns—
*Don't drop them, they were your grandmother's you know.*

The mind sees a dark stick in the water and it no longer
sees the stick, it sees the snake,
no, not even the snake but the painful bites—
first the leg, then the arm and finally
a nest of them on your stomach and
before you realize why, you are slapping at
water and air, moving as fast as you can
away from a branch drifting calmly toward
the dock.

My brain watched my husband and son swimming,
a storm on the way, the water stirred-up and nauseous,
and suddenly my mind has destroyed them both.
The yellow blanket whipped away, the beach ball
whipped beyond reach, everything moving too fast—
paint on silk—the clouds, my family,
the beautiful colors bleeding quietly
and out of control somewhere downstream.

And then we are a family once more.
I am taking them a towel and begging them
to get out before it's too late.
If the brain has too much free time, it stays busy

all day burying and resurrecting what it cannot bear
and what it cannot bear to lose.

## *Shell Necklace*

I wore them again today
without knowing why.
They pinch and rub like grains of sand
caught like memory
between right brain and left.
Or I fumble them like worry beads
between forefinger and thumb,
three sets of five decades
an eternity of small shells
until they become dumb to the touch—
like artificial light in a sunfilled room—
unnecessary and costly.

*Hail Mary full of grace*
*Blessed art thou among sinners,*
*Blessed is the fruit of thy womb.*

Butterfly shells caught
and threaded on fish line—
five of this color
then five clumped together,
a vacant star,
shell-shocked.
This morning everything,
even God,
rises and falls into the sea.

If chance has wrapped this primitive rosary
about my neck, I try to welcome it.
Try to forget the dark-haired boy
who dug shells all morning for well-dressed tourists,
and strung them not by some romantic moon

but by electric light—
realistic and painful
in its simple, unadorned state.
My only sin was paying what he asked.

I take them off tonight
without knowing why.
The largest shell which curls inside itself
like memory, distorted and true only to itself,
knocked against my heart all morning.

# *Against All Desire*

1

For weeks now, desire. Impatient and thick-lipped
as locusts, free at last, after fourteen years
unearthed and airborne.
A sore that has festered and fed on the damp-dark
excursions of body minus soul.

The bleached-dry bones of Georgia O'Keefe's desert
wink and shift, a restless lover.
Hundreds of skulls painted over and over,
altered and sensuous again on canvas
and still
the land is not satisfied
and vomits up another.
She carries it back to her studio like a nun.

I can't make it better and I can't decide
which-is-which realistic version
and so I sit looking out the window:
a head pops out of a head.
A white-faced monkey nuzzles the philosopher's shoulder,
all of a piece—the beauty of art.
I sit on the sofa like a nun.

2

The hardest poems to write
are the ones I stuff in my pocket
like seeds a young child saves
without stopping to think.
Paper fortunes scraped from the table

and told to no one.

I hold on because I believe in charms.
Faust, for all his knowledge, kissed the devil
full on the lips. Outrageous sickness
passed on like measles and I want to be propped
in bed—pillows fluffed, sheets billowing and blending
with real clouds, enjoying this itch more than
relief.

Unformed. Featureless. Darkness
flowers desire. Smooth
as my aunt's long legs
stretched out and deeply tanned,
Helen of Troy burning slowly
inside a body barely alive . . .
like a nun . . . sometimes . . . .

Sandra Agricola was born in Mobile, Alabama, in 1956. She grew up in Georgia and Alabama and uses the landscape of these two states to create her own vision of the South. She received her B.A. from the University of Alabama and her M.A. in English from Ohio University. *Master Bedroom Poems* is her first collection. She lives with her husband and son in Jackson, Mississippi.